DONALD
and the
GOLDEN
CRAYON

#45

By P. Shauers

SCHIFFER
PUBLISHING

4880 Lower Valley Road
Atglen, PA 19310

Type set in DTLAlbertinaST/FrysBaskerville BT

ISBN: 978-0-7643-5655-1
Printed in the United States of America

Published by Schiffer Publishing, Ltd.
4880 Lower Valley Road
Atglen, PA 19310
Phone: (610) 593-1777; Fax: (610) 593-2002
Info@schifferbooks.com
www.schifferbooks.com

In the middle of the night, Donald woke from his terrific sleep and cried out, "Covfefe!"

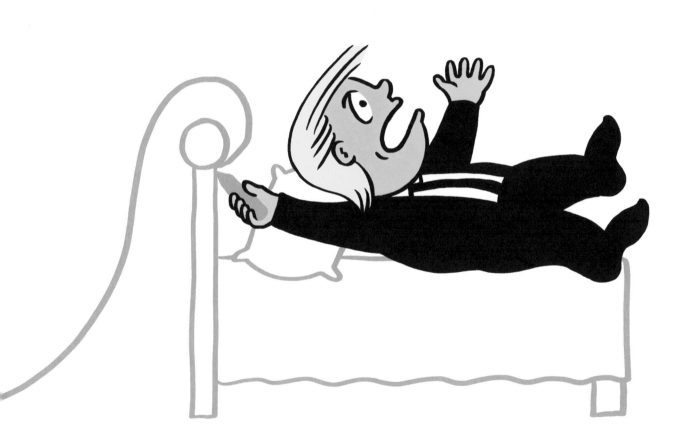

Now that he was wide awake, Donald decided that he wanted to play golf. Using his amazing golden crayon, Donald drew a hill, and then another, and soon he had a golf course.

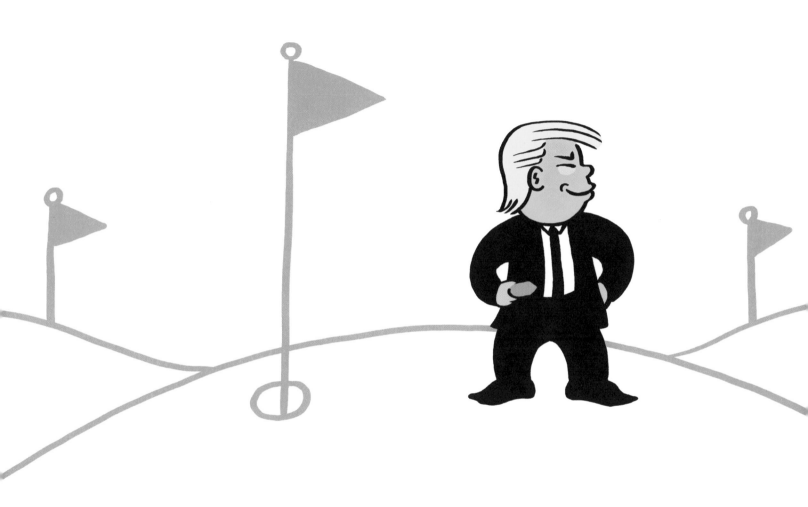

It was the best golf course ever. Tremendous golf course.

Donald saw that there were people running across his golf course. Bad people. They didn't look like him. They were from shithole countries.

He started building a wall. Brick by brick, it went up
and up, and soon it was done. It was a terrific wall.

Donald admired his tremendous wall. He made a door and went through it. On the other side of the wall was a fantastic crowd.

Great people. A yuge crowd. They all love Donald. They all looked like
Donald, and they too hated people from shithole countries.

Everything was great until a weak group of morons showed up. They were haters who didn't love Donald. A terrible, terrible riot started.

There were good people on both sides.
So sad. Donald made another door.
A very good door.

The door led to a secret room. It had many beeping cybers and a huge nuclear button. It was a very big nuclear button. The biggest nuclear button anywhere.

But what's the point of having nuclears if we can't use them, thought Donald.

He climbed a ladder out of the secret room and came out right into
a Native American reservation. Another shithole. Sad.

He ran a pipeline made of beautiful steel, beautiful Russian steel, right through it. So much winning.

Tired of walking, Donald made a boat and passed some houses that were underwater. People who did not vote for Donald said it was climate change.

Wrong! Climate change is a hoax created by the Chi-neese.

Donald noticed the water was clean. Really clean. He opened
a coal factory that would spill all sorts of crap right into it.

It's going to make lots of money. Which is really, really great.

He passed a city destroyed by a hurricane. They had
no water and no electricity. They asked him for help.

Donald said they wanted everything to be done for them. Sorry, losers.

Donald found a hospital, but it was filled with germs and
disgusting blood. He kept walking.

Nobody knew healthcare was so complicated.

Donald wanted everyone to know how great America is, so he made the greatest military parade ever. Tremendous parade! Yuge!

He filled the parade with soldiers that he liked because they weren't captured.
He didn't have to march because he had a heel spur.

Next, Donald invented the Space Force.
It's like the Air Force, but in space. Space Force.

At first, he was not really serious about it, then decided it was a great idea. Space Force!

Donald was growing tired. Very tired.

He made a cozy little place to sleep.

Inside, there were lots and lots of rooms, let me tell you.

He soon found out which room was his because he was
one of the smartest people anywhere in the world.

His room was beautiful, just beautiful. It had beautiful golden curtains, a tremendous golden statue, and a wonderful golden bed.

It even had a steamy golden shower.

Donald was lonely in his golden palace, so he pushed a special button.

A secret door opened up and Donald's friend came in.

Oops! Wrong button.

He pushed another button and his sexy friend came in.

Moments later, Donald was so exhausted and thirsty.
He pushed a third special button.

He got a Diet Coke and the most beautiful piece of chocolate cake you've ever seen.

Now he wanted to relax and watch TV.

But Donald did not like what was on, so he drew another TV.

Donald hated the dishonest media.

So dishonest.

He threw his golden crayon at the pathetic TVs.

And the crayon broke in half.

 **DONALD**

What loser invented crayons? Too weak.
They break too easily. So sad.

After accomplishing so much, Donald was
exhausted and went to sleep.

As he drifted off, he cried out, "Covfefe" once again . . .